rivers...

    and other blackness

        ...between us

other works by
d'bi.young.anitafrika

art on black
blood.claat

rivers...
and other blackness
...between us

(dub) poems of love

d'bi.young.anitafrika

Women's Press
Toronto

rivers... and other blackness... between us
d'bi.young.anitafrika

First published in 2007 by
Women's Press, an imprint of Canadian Scholars' Press Inc.
180 Bloor Street West, Suite 801
Toronto, Ontario
M5S 2V6

www.womenspress.ca

Copyright © 2007 d'bi.young.anitafrika and Canadian Scholars' Press Inc. All rights reserved. No part of this publication may be photocopied, reproduced, stored in a retrieval system, or transmitted, in any form or by any means, electronic, mechanical, or otherwise, without the written permission of Canadian Scholars' Press, except for brief passages quoted for review purposes. In the case of photocopying, a licence may be obtained from Access Copyright: One Yonge Street, Suite 1900, Toronto, Ontario, M5E 1E5, (416) 868-1620, fax (416) 868-1621, toll-free 1-800-893-5777, www.accesscopyright.ca.

Every reasonable effort has been made to identify copyright holders. Canadian Scholars' Press would be pleased to have any errors or omissions brought to its attention.

Canadian Scholars' Press/Women's Press gratefully acknowledges financial support for our publishing activities from the Ontario Arts Council, the Canada Council for the Arts, the Government of Canada through the Book Publishing Industry Development Program (BPIDP), and the Government of Ontario through the Ontario Book Publishing Tax Credit Program.

Library and Archives Canada Cataloguing in Publication
d'bi.young.anitafrika, 1977-
    Rivers– and other blackness– between us : (dub) poems of love / d'bi.young.anitafrika.
ISBN 978-0-88961-463-5
    I. Title.
PS8607.B55R59 2007   C811'.6   C2007-906156-7

Cover and interior design: Aldo Fierro

Cover art: *indigo woman*; part one: *she's sweet like mangoes*; part two: *emotions*; part three: *alive*. Art by Suritah Wignall. Reproduced by permission of the artist. www.sweetlikemangoe.com.

Back cover background: "Red textured wall surface." © Bill Noll. iStockphoto 2867171

10   11   5   4   3   2

Printed and bound in Canada by Marquis Book Printing Inc.

   Canada Council   Conseil des Arts   Canada
                       for the Arts   du Canada

to you
young black boys in my life
moon
johari
tremaine
love makes the world go round

gryphen
I am forever changed
by (y)our love

to those whom I have loved
and who have loved me
this is an offering

is love an art? then it requires knowledge and effort. or is love a pleasant sensation, which to experience is a matter of chance, something one "falls into" if one is lucky?

—erich fromm

contents

one: rivers...

yellow • 2

young black • 3

city of (brotherly) love • 9

bible and gun • 10

shakespeare (i) • 12

foolishness • 13

shakespeare (ii) • 16

revolushun (ii) • 17

desire • 19

dear mama • 20

sistahly solidarity • 23

politricks • 24

track and field • 26

there she goes—womban in high • 27

two: and other blackness

we tellin' stories yo • 32

untitled (i) • 34

non-reality of past tense • 35

holy • 36

pretend there are no lines • 39

by boat • 40

singularity • 41

bloodlines • 45

self-esteem (ii) • 46

foreign mind/local body • 47

he said… • 50

comfortable wid me • 51

common sense • 53

two truths • 54

luna • 55

duality on a binary fetus (i) • 57

in honour of belief • 58

snake tongue • 60

three: ...between us

this... • 62

dear black lover friend • 63

ase • 66

night's moon • 67

when the love is not enough:
    the conversation I never had with billie holiday • 68

(post)colonial blues • 74

duality on a binary fetus (ii) • 75

blood orange • 76

(w)hole • 78

love speak • 79

praise song for mengesha (i) • 80

praise song for mengesha (ii) • 83

untitled (ii) • 84

little sistah • 85

delusions and grandeur • 87

seven generashuns • 88

an olive branch • 91

rivers and other blackness between us • 93

one
rivers…

yellow
to madre ochun

your kindness
winds
bends
offers up
an ocean
endless
rivers of possibilities
flow downstream

ochun meets yemaya
at the elegua of love

young black
for moon and da urban griots

young black girl said I have to tell you something
don't believe them when they try to put you
in a box
and leave you there to rot
you can give the world a talk
walk yuh walk
young black boy said I have to tell you something
you are brilliant and beautiful and
strong and rare
do anything you dare
you can teach the world your truth
dig yuh roots

because I am more than the roundness of my ass
the width of my tits
the thickness of my thighs
the depths of my hips
the glimmity-glammity hold him tight
all through the night
is not necessarily my numbah-one priority

because I play ball like a ballah
my body sculpted pre centuries of mule-hauling
cotton sugar cane-picking

my own grave digging
does not mean
my only dream
is to become a *basketball star*
a *track-and-field negro*
or *soul-singing sambo*
I can be an athlete or storyteller if I choose
knowing these are NOT my only options

I am young and black and brilliant
my ancestors: rebellious and stubborn and resilient
build on their backs
bloodlines of futures insistent
on survival
I redefine your *tribal*
box
and encourage you to get corrective lenses
so you can truly see me

we
walking through metal detectors in school
that refuse to detect the rape and pillage
recolonized by the great
harris-tocracy
we
experiencing
the military's militarization
of high school and middle school education
police officers turned hall monitors

like the war on terror
this war is actually a war on people
warmongers terrorizing youth
of colour
not for oil
but for the future

prime directive—preserve the white façade
cuz *brown* and *yellow* and *black* and *red* populations
are growing
exponentially
spilling over the multi-culti melting pot
and *we need to keep the natives off the land*
and the immigrants beyond the borders
and if that doesn't work
suspend them from school then
and if that *doesn't work*
expel them from school
and if that *still* doesn't work
fuck then just close the fucking school
send them to learn a trade instead
streamlined math and english
f class
no university for you
cuz you our underclass
a new generation of worker ants
while we ignore them sending mostly poor young
red, black, yellow, brown, and *white* children to die at war

young black girl said I have to tell you something
to survive these times you gotta be
strong of mind
don't be afraid to shine
hold your head up high and stride
walk with pride
young black boy said I have to tell you something
I know it takes a lot to become a man
sometimes it's hard to find
a good foundation
be your own example son
refuse their guns

after-school projects cut
while you make
projects out of our neighbourhoods
and perpetu(h)ate
the new apartheid genocide
or move us out of our neighbourhoods
and cre(h)ate
the new apartment gentrified
recreation centres. art programs. extracurricular activities
replaced by what: malls and prisons and prozac and suicide
police gun suppliers supplying
young black brilliant
dealers and buyers
of an old white boys' club economy

whether its crack cocaine or cotton
we steady picking picking picking

and somebody steady reaping reaping reaping
black mother steady weeping
because my brother's dead
or inna jail
or inna madhouse
or him just hang himself
and my sister she just been beat up
or gang-raped
or diagnosed as manic depressive
or she just jumped the trax or the 401
yo

we want more than malls and prisons and prozac and suicide
and 10:30 curfews and coca-cola happy meals
or the latest escapist joyride
because we are not *happy*
we are young and black and brilliant
and we want more than a piece of dry-up canadian apple pie
infested with smallpox hepatitis aids-tainted blood

young black girl said I have to tell you something
you have a right to liberashun
you have a right to self-protekshun
you have a right to happiness and
love inna di land
young black boy said I have to tell you something
you haffi fi fight dem segregashun
fight dem criminalizashun
demand respect and admirashun
and love inna di land

because you are young
and black
and brilliant
and afrikan
and canadian
and caribbean
and european
and south asian
and south east asian
and east asian
and south american
and first nations
and beautiful
and girl and boy
and because I love you
young black boy
said I have to tell you something
young black girl
said I have to tell you something
you are why I sing

city of (brotherly) love

black people and beauty
are not a struggled affair
I wanted to give the brother
with the lox
a memory

black stilettos
blue pants
yellow copper sunset bra
ethiopian circles
and smiles to drown sorrow

he touched my hand
attempting to heal wounds
hidden from the pale naked eye

brother-man took me up
not to create hierarchies
but to re-love
black wombanhood
and blackness

bible and gun

dem cum wid a bible and a gun
dem cum wid shackles and rum
dem cum singing *god save di queen*
god will save you too if yuh down pon yuh knees
fi 500 years
blood sweat and tears
convert di afrikans
brainwash di afrikans
his eye is on di sparrow
misogynist missionary work
what a insanity
inna di name of christianity
moddah country want to boost har economy
suh now you are a colony
existing fi feed white supremacy
slave labour or indian indenture
while yuh bow an scrape to a eurocentric faith
stolen from ethiopia
ripped from di womb of mama afrika
my people a time fi remembah

rise up black people rise up
time to break dese chains
christianity was used to enslave we
time dat we are free

I say rise up black people rise up
time to break dese chains
our spirits have been living in captivity
time to set dem free

gimme mawu elegua nu kwa
gimme yoruba ochun yemoja
gimme akan ifa obatala
gimme di moon and di star
gimme di water and di plants
respect for all living life
gimme di people an di sun
afro-spiritual tradishun

shakespeare (i)
to nancy palk

black (k)night
blue moon
red sun
blood's bloom
secret flower
passion's eye
winged hosanna
enchanted lyre
lucid breath
illusive thought
waking dream
walking laugh
here today
future's call
circles path
mirrored wall

foolishness
for jason harrow

bwoy a peer foolishness a gwaan
inna dis place enuh
if we waan tings fi change
we haffi mek haste enuh
we nuh ave nuh time
fi waste enuh

mi membah when mi did deh a jamaica
ghetto life nevah fun
seh when mi come a foreign
nuff tings a guh run
den mi walk down di street
an a sistren see mi
seh she cyaan't even greet
nah look inna mi yeye
I am di colour of her skin
when she look pon mi
she see herself within

foolishness

deh a school di oddah day
a mine mi own bizniz
some people cum beside me

suh mi get inquisitive
overhear a girl seh
mi faadah get lay-off yesterday
trouble fi di family
boss seh im fire
im cum home an beat him dawtah
angry at each oddah
instead of at our oppressah

foolishness

mi siddung fi watch a tv program
some hype music pon a b.e.t. station
bwoy an gyal jus a wine dem bottom
nutten nuh wrong
den mi realize
dem a advatize
cyar an liquor
an nuff nuff lies
telling me what it's really like
in *da hood*
people drunk an rich
an life is good

foolishness

guh a meeting fi black people
some canadian caribbean afrikan an american
nuh baddy naw listen to dem one anoddah

a peer division
real unity nuh mean unanimity
unity mean finding solidarity
among our differences
it is necessary
suh if peaches have a plan
you have anoddah one
nuh baddah mind
membah
black people are not a homogeneous nation
we need nuff strategy
fi find a solushun
nuff strategy fi mek revolushun

mi membah when mi did deh a jamaica
ghetto life nevah fun
seh when mi come a foreign
nuff tings a guh run
but
bwoy a peer foolishness a gwaan
inna dis place enuh
if we waan fi mek change
we haffi mek haste enuh
we nuh ave nuh time fi waste

shakespeare (ii)
to lászló marton

a black dove
pursues the dragon
surrenderously
part snaked, part monstered, part winged
these creatures of grounded flight
swoon!

heresy! heresy!

the world about me is upturned
this dragon's speak
makes wells of dams of my well-being
shape-shifting of an extraordinary kind
devours what I knew of myself
yesterday

revolushun (ii)
inspired by dennis brown

do you know what it means
to have a revolushun

mi waan fi ask we black people
if we ave amneshah
inna jamaica everybody a fallah
di u.s. of imperialist amerikkka
waan fi lef di island guh a foreign guh suffah

amerikkkan dream is what we a defen
nobody nuh remembah way back when
di maroons did fight against wi enslavement
kill off di dyam english spanish and french
send dem back weh dem come from
gain independence
united we stan
di divided mus repent

suh where di british leave off
di amerikkkans start
want a new playground
when cuba kick dem rass
going all around di world
selling amerikkkan dreams
jamaicans don't buy dis babylonian scheme

amerikkka tief di resources and di lan—dem suh bold
export crack cocaine fi kill di young and di old
biggest arms smuggler pon disya world scene
dem gi wi pickney big gun
fi kill dem bright ghetto dream

politician doan give a shit about di state a di country
dem sell-out to amerikkka fi mek nuff money
bogus election wid only two party
ave jamaican kill jamaican while dem feel hawty
if yuh walk pon di street whole heap a starving pickney
government yuh a provide any opportunity?
people mus ave access to basic necessity
only a revolushun
only a revolushun
only a revolushun
will end disya poverty

do you know what it means
to have a revolushun
to make a solushun
to save fi wi nashun

desire
for jacob c(h)ino

infatuated
I told the rivers (and other blackness)
I compete with the madness of your currents
quickened by love

dear mama
inspired by sonny's lettah
for l.k.j.

dear mama
good aftanoon
I hope you are happy and well
I have something I have to tell
you...

how is auntie sarah
and uncle mike
cousin ivan
and next-door neighbour
what's her name again
bulah
I hope they are happy and well
I miss them

mama
I have something I have to tell
you...

I know yuh send me to canada
to learn a trade
yuh send me to canada to make a good grade
yuh send me to canada to get a betta life
no more strife no more struggles
inna we life
right?

dear mama
nine months ago today

I went to the doctor
to get the results of an
hiv
test
mama I really really really did try mi best
but I know that yuh won't be impressed
with the news

the doctor him say I positive

my friends and them
they used to laugh
say the gay white fags
they have no class
and that is why
god punish them
and give them aids
right inna dem ass

I have a boyfriend mama
it's not only gay people get this mama
i'm black and straight mama
hiv don't discriminate mama
hiv don't discriminate

one night I felt lonely
I called up charmaine
and told her the story

then she told pat
pat told michael
michael told linda
linda told john
and the whole of them
treating me
like a dirty diseased womban

now my friends and dem
won't talk to me
won't drink from my cup
won't touch me
won't kiss me goodbye won't hug me
won't let me babysit their pickney

now I know how it feel
when my friends and dem laugh
at the gay white fags
saying they have no class
I feel like god is punishing me
and give me aids right inna my ass

mama I want to come home
only you alone can love me
but yuh have to promise
that yuh won't tell nobady
about my shame…
not
auntie sarah
uncle mike
not cousin ivan
or the neighbour bulah

please keep it
as our little secret

your loving daughter
…

sistahly solidarity
for staceyann chin

brown dirt
clothed in black
breathes cool air
and cool pose
my son shining like a brown sun
on the cusp of two and manhood

mommy writes of androgyne
and other mystics

dreams in purple solstices
and staceyanns
and revolushun
and womben
and men

politricks
to stephen harper

mi dream last night
bout one game name
piss pon di people politricks
di objective
stand up pon di highest building
gather as many people as possible
below
pull out your penis and piss and piss and piss
far far far and wide wide wide
(womben need not enter)
di man on di tallest building
who pisses di farthest
and on as many people as possible
is the *prime-winner*
mi have a dream last night

mi dream last night bout dis
gated condominium community
a funeral procession of benz, bmw, jaguar, and lexus
driving through di sky-high great—wall—of—china long fence
celebrating di death of
womban's rites. abortion. gay marriage. daycare. public education
public health care. public housing. public hydro
in fact everyting public

poor people. homeless people. some of colour. differently able. and first
nations people
like animals on a farm in the year 1984
caged in bantuland reservashuns
each subdivision armed wid an electric chair for public execushun

mi have a dream last night
dat some man did a play a game wid mi life

mi wake up and ask myself dis mawning
what is crucial in dis fast becoming police state of emergency
survival
human equality
deciding what happens in my own body
human equality
more access fi different people
human equality
power as social safety
net
human equality
dreaming widout fear
of returning to a nightmare
di old boys' piss-pon-di-people club
called history

mi wake up dis morning
harper
did
win

track and field

ready. set. go
this discombobulated relay
of
words
tripping over sentences
that
lie like cane-rows
in the field

there she goes—womban in high
for our sister andrea who jumped
and her son who went before her

there she goes
splinters pounding paces of melancholy
spread across the bare of breasts
dripping drops of danger
a refusal to regret
duality hard like rock-stone
and jackass corn
wedged in cracks of creases
of flailing nostrils
and sailed relationships
she wants to say *I hate*
but knows that mirrors know no end
and tell lies
while they are honest
fuck me beyond remembrance
a sea-saw of pleasure and pain
is neutrality
deniable
smoke, shrooms, alcohol
and a highway of concrete promises
metal in transition
a nose-dive into taboos
with a two-year-old black boy
black mother—where is your lover?

it's all too much too much too much too much too much too much
much too much too much too much too much too much too much
too much too much too much too much too much too much too much
much too much too much too much too much too much too much
too much too much too much too much too much too much too much
much too much too much too much too much too much too much
too much too much too much too much too much too much too much
much too much too much too much too much too much too much
too much too much too much too much too much too much too much
much too much too much too much too much too much too much
too much too much too much too much too much too much too much
much too much too much too much too much too much too much
too much too much too much too much too much too much too much
much too much too much too much too much too much too much
too much too much too much too much too much too much too much
much too much too much too much too much too much too much
too much too much too much too much too much too much too much
much too much too much too much too much too much too much
too much too much too much too much too much too much too much
much too much too much too much too much too much too much
too much too much too much too much too much too much too much
too much too much too much too much too much too much too much
muchtoo much too much too much too much too much too much too
too much too much too much too much too much too much too much
much too much too much too much too much too much too much
too much too much too much too much too much too much too much
much too much too much too much too much too much too much

o much too much too much too much too much too much too much too
o much too much too much too much too much too much too much too much
h too much too much too much too much too much too much too much too
o much too much too much too much too much too much too much too much
h too much too much too much too much too much too much too much too
o much too much too much too much too much too much too much too much
h too much too much too much too much too much too much too much too
o much too much too much too much too much too much too much too much
h too much too much too much too much too much too much too much too
o much too much too much too much too much too much too much too much
h too much too much too much too much too much too much too much too
o much too much too much too much too much too much too much too much
h too much too much too much too much too much too much too much too
o much too much too much too much too much too much too much too much
h too much too much too much too much too much too much too much too
o much too much too much too much too much too much too much too much
h too much too much too much too much too much too much too much too
o much too much too much too much too much too much too much too much
h too much too much too much too much too much too much too much too
o much too much too much too much too much too much too much too much
h too much too much too much too much too much too much too much
h too much too much too much too much too much too much too much too
o much too much too much too much too much too much too much too much
h too much too much too much too much too much too much too much too
o much too much too much too much too much too much too much too much
h too much too much too much too much too much too much too much too
o much too much too much too much too much too much too much too much

two
and other blackness

we tellin' stories yo
for magia and alex

the storytellers are the keepers of the scroll
the keepers of the truth
the keepers of the legacy

when we disrespect the stories
we disregard a herstory our history
built on the blood
built on the blood
build on the blood
of the backs of dem warriors
amazon fighters
mothers and fathers
daughters
children of black people

modern griots I charge you to
reflect the truth
reflection
like yemaya/olokun
seeing her perfect black self
in atlantic ocean waters
where the bravest reside

modern griots I urge you to
reflect the truth
reflection

hiphoppers
dubpoets/spoken word artists
playwrights/writers/actors/dancers/politicians
painters

find the poetry that reflects integrity
find the poetry that reflects integrity
there is a world community
that you could give a shit about

who is the overseer in this time
give an mc who has no integrity
a mic
and s/he will rhyme
the death of the people

untitled (i)

shoulders broad
even
for balance
not hunched nor arched
no slimmer look

hands dem calloused
never worked in the fields
this is genetic

feet wide
spread
fi balance

legs strong
strong as an ox

new black
womanhood
old as time

non-reality of past tense

futures passed
these bruised lips

why un-realize dreams
crippled fear
becoming man
beautiful womban

holy
for pecola breedlove

when janey was five
she used to catch fireflies
she used to put dem inna bokkle
an cork it

den she walk roun in di dark
jus fi see di fire start
janey eye dem get white
as di bokkle burn bright

now janey turn eight
but she graduate late
she jus a start grade one
wid har likkle frien sam

janey janey
peenie wallie
twinkling star
look like yuh coming
from lands afar

inna primary school
pickney mus play by di rule
dem fit janey wid a dunce cap
dem laugh an seh she handicap

she is di oldest inna class
janey always guh a class
five days a week
janey nevah turn weak

all di boys an all di girls
tease janey call har fool
dem seh handicap people
mus guh to a speshal school
a yuh moddah tell yuh dat
or a yuh faadah tell yuh dat
janey ask di pickney dem
dem seh *yes an so what*

janey janey
peenie wallie
twinkling star
look like yuh coming
from lands afar

one day pon di playground
sam an im frien dem surround
janey by harself
and dem fight har down

dem tump har in har head
dem jook har in har eye
dem laugh an run away
dem leave janey to die

now at twenty-five
janey cannot open her eyes
all she see is peenie wallie
all she hear are fireflies

pretend there are no lines

halfway house
dem theories
to blow

intellect
most wanted
while a seeker
sinks in quicksand

oh I wish I could
cry
I would weep

by boat
for madre yemaya

riding crevices
blue
and white

pulse
sucked
into
smooth
tonites

singularity

tell me why is it dat
at a party
everybody jolly an hearty
i'm sitting on a stool
denying dis loneliness

girl yuh's an only child
yuh's a fortunate child
yuh's a privilege child
yuh's an intelligent child
so why don't yuh smile for a while
an give your face a rest

yes I will smile for many whiles
an pledge a prayer of pretense
so I could exist in the present
live my pseudo experience
reconfirm existence

yes I will smile
no I will laugh
ha ha
laughter is the weapon of fools

I will laugh
find humour
inna any sorta blunder
humour in pride
humour in genocide
humour in suicide
laugh for many whiles
though under black blubber skin
blood boils an bleeds
for a break of monotony

suicide/singularity
suicide/singularity
suicide/singularity

is eating me from the insides
is eating me from the outsides
is eating me from all sides

run ghana run
run from dem white walls
stiff as stone
a try trap yuh inna dem cell
dem institution
run from machine pave foundation
dat a alienate yuh from di rest of dem
run from discomfort pain loneliness want want of sex want of food
run from people who want acceptance
run from di ting
wid two han
two leg

a head
an no name
run from you

mama yuh had mi
mama yuh didn't plan
fi start yuh family dis early
but yuh had mi
one month two month three month to nine
mama yuh mek mi invade yuh space an force yuh outta shape
physical an emotional pain
she fifteen an she breeding
nutten will come of dat girl
shame on di family but yuh had mi
going an coming from school wid a expanding belly
mama couldn't hide nausea sickness self-hate
but yuh had mi

do you know that you spend
as much as
one million dollars
on raising a child?
only until the little brats are sixteen though
with a university education
you can spend an additional
two million dollars
after that just pray they get a good job
live out a quiet existence
they're quite an unsafe investment
what with accidental deaths
and god forbid

suicide
personally I think a dog is a safer bet

mama yuh didn't plan
to start yuh family
dis early but
I remember yuh tell mi yuh
yuh get a blessing from di skies
mama yuh wise

yes
I consented
though I could see a thousand futures
exacting earth's murmur pulse
a lull
I consented
though I could taste zinc rust in the belly of my throat
smell rotting shantytowns beckoning at my feet
I consented
though I could see you my denied daughter
holding fast to your decayed father
hear you my child
wailing burning bright
wanting to be held for the first time

mama yuh had mi
mama hol mi fi di first time

mi mus fight dis lack of clarity
mus fight dis singularity
run ghana run

bloodlines

blood dried
through my veins

no more
will they bleed

like a rotting carcass
I feel micro
biotic
squirlies
squiggling
below the surface of my skin

low hemoglobin
anemia
or madness

to comfort myself
I thought
of frida

self-esteem (ii)

paranoia
has
lessened
since
my
return

work makes
normal
people
of us all

foreign mind/local body
for n.k.m.

me friend deh a foreign fi di last two weeks
one place call montreal
everytime mi ask har if dat mean seh
she deh close to brooklyn new york
she tell me seh she nuh know
well foreign a foreign
an who cyaan guh a foreign a bat
me dun know seh
me have one whole heap a family a foreign
me have family a florida
a atlanta
even a new york
me have family inna a brooklyn
nyc represent!
well mi best friend
we been bes friend fi
mek me see
bout thirteen years
since wi a three years old
we used to give each oddah everyting
from ice cream
to blouse and skirt
to book and pencil
wi did even guh a di same basic school together

me best friend tell me dat
when she get pan har feet at
foreign
she a sen mi new shoes
and clothes
and nuff panty an brief
well di brief dem a fi mi breddah jacob,
him a seven now
just turn seven last week

mi hear seh foreign nice enuh
tings free
di street dem pave wid gold
and money grow pon tree basically
yuh tink inna foreign people live inna zinc house
a brick dem live inna
like inna di story book dem
hansel and gretel
people nuh live inna poverty and degradation like we do
all di cussing and fighting
looting and murdering nuh gwaan a foreign
inna jam dung life hard
an people wi do anyting fi backbite yuh

inna foreign
everybody live inna one white picket fence
wid house
and land and cyar
and dog

and two point three pickney
dem even have washing machine and dryer
dem even have machine fi wash up dem cup and plate
a laziness dat if yuh ask me
but nobody nevah ask

mi soon gawn a foreign
but me best friend gone quicker dan mi

but wait how come she
nuh write mi back yet
after she dun tell me seh
she is me bes frien
yuh know weh dem seh bout people like dat
dem get rich an switch
yes
she gawn a foreign and get rich and switch

he said...

beauty is
imperfection
some poet once told

I am forced to
learn
perfection's veil
has lifted

comfortable wid me
for mengesha

I want to be comfortable wid me
mi waan fi be comfortable inna me
a di end a di day
nobady nuh lef
but me and mi gawdess
mi waan fi be di me
who she create
comfortable inna me

when mi feel jealousy
mi own insecurity
if yuh nah see mi beauty
mi start tink seh mi ugly

but you have weh you have
an me have weh me have
mi start tink seh mi nuh have
cuz mi nuh have weh you have

suh mi gi yuh mi power
den self-loathing mi devour
is jus lack a introspecshun
a maintain mi oppreshun

mi aguh stop tink
inna dem paradigms
get my mind unintertwined
from the shackles of dem chains
mi use a eternity fi hate me
now mi a see
why mi deyah again

I want to be comfortable wid me
mi waan fi be comfortable inna me
a di end a di day
nobady nuh lef
but me and mi gawdess
mi waan fi be di me
who she create
comfortable wid me
comfortable inna me

common sense

perspective creeps
haunts me
like a
soucouyant

two truths

is love
truth
shaped by you
retouched by your lover
retouched by you
reshaped by your lover
reshaped by you
retouched…
until the difference
between two
truths
is an infinite
mirror

luna

last night la luna she came to me
and while I slept she spoke to me
she said: I am crying tears of blue
she said: I am shining yet I cannot see you,
my children why

are all my rivers dry
you suck my blood/my oil/you toxify
the earth
my sky is crowded with clouds of pain
you rape my trees my plants
what do you stand to gain

what have you done with tomorrow
what will you do with today
yesterday's future is hurting
while this night turns to day

have you forgotten where you come from
birthed from my moon womb divine
fifty-two stars
you steal the souls of this time
stars birthed from blood
my children do not shine

what have you done with tomorrow
what will you do with today
yesterday's future is hurting
while this night turns to day
my children
this night turns to day
I am slipping away

duality on a binary fetus (i)

hide in me
thick night

...stifling...

her blanket
protects
me
from myself

in honour of belief
for trey anthony and da kink collective

in all parts of di world
live a little boy a little girl
who is crying for a mommy for a daddy
for an auntie for an uncle for a granny
who is crying for a brotha a sistah a friend
to defend them from
di deep bitter bile
violating hands dat creep
beneath di sheet
when dem a sleep
dis secret (secret)
a monster inna di closet

little girl little boy di moon is your witness
dis sickness
is no fault of yours
we carry di karmic shame
for not stepping in
and now you are to blame
little boy little girl di moon is your witness

little boy little girl di moon is your witness
dis sickness is no fault of yours
we carry di karmic scar

for not stepping in before it went too far
little girl little boy di moon is your witness

now di time has come
get off of di ground
no more a little girl a little boy
you are a womban you are a man
stand up strong

turn your face to the moon
and your spirit to the sun
and you SHINE without SHAME
this story is yours and mine to claim

little boy di moon is your witness
little girl the moon is your witness
little boy the moon is your witness
little girl the moon
the blue blue moon
is your witness
the moon is your witness
the moon is your witness

snake tongue
for raphael cohen

was it a snake
or winding
that lay some bare kiss
of inevitability
in their crossing
elegua called
a red-headed boy
a red-tempered girl
to lay offerings
at his feet
and so they did

sacrificial lambs
of experiential knowledge
choose knowingly
choose wisely
choose love

three
...between us

this…
for m.b.

this touch tastes
sweet
like brown sugar
pon tamarind ball
in a saturday afternoon
wid di sun
high inna di sky
and hot-a-fire
bright and brilliant
jus a shine pon mi

blue black mountain
lips
marooned on the slopes
of my beckoning, part

an utterance of
change
licks a whisper, wet and
dark
between erect valleys
of my womb—
an(d)—other—hooded things
becoming the edge of my desire

I surrender silence to the timelessness of you

dear black lover friend

I am writing because in speaking I may not be as honest
I know I promised *drama-free* but
that's hard for a drama queen

what happened with my son tonite
shook my very core
I chose to ignore my spirit when she said
he's sick today. stay home and nurse him. he needs you
instead I continued with my contract gig
and asked a friend to care for him
just two minutes before me getting through the door
he breaks his head open

I am being triggered from all angles
from my mommy having been a performer
and not having been there sometimes
to my daddy choosing to not be there most times
to having to go to work
even though my baby is sick
because we need the money
and mommy needs to work

I went to the hospital tonite
and it hurt like hell

what does a mother do for her wounded child
particularly fearing that physical scars heal
while emotional ones deepen with age
I know
I am twenty-eight and that chip on my shoulder still bleeds

what does this have to do with you
with us
well
until a few weeks ago
I was content with *no significant other*
living my own convictions
here you come with all your beauty and intelligence
and humour and sex and love
and I love you

the wise ones say
wish carefully...

lover
I am a single working queer artist mother
who thought I was ready to love three ways
but tonite at the hospital
I realized that barely am I loving two ways
let alone three
I felt/feel broken and sad
that ochun has offered
and I am not ready

the truth about how I feel is this:
I am parenting my son solo by a thin thread of time
I love him
I am somewhat managing to take him to school
to pick him up from school
to make his food
to go to work
by the time I am done
there is hardly time to play with him
take him to the park

how can I offer love to someone else when
I am not even managing the responsibilities
that come with being someone's mother
I know I am no martyr but I feel I can do better
if I try harder
I have got to try harder

I have heard people talk about how challenging it is
to have children and then try having a partner as well
it works with support and balance and time
I don't have the hang of it yet

if we are to be together
some more time apart
won't hurt…

ase

thank eshu
god
allah
goddess
jesus
shango
buddha
yemaya
sun-ra
nu kwa
life force
ochun
universe
water
oya
mountains
wind
obatala
and moon
ancestors
ogun
krishna…

for you

night's moon

2:45 a.m.
a night of rhythm
pounding pavement
dub
dancing with boys young enough to
be older than my brother
on sharp sweet
edges of manhood
and manic desires…
smiling with girls
who want to be caressed
by gentle boyish-girl hands
deep dark and calloused
wanting me to shave just one
layer of whiteness
off their prodigal past
I understand both these desperations

me
longing for consumption
in the abyss of you
remembering passion
a three-way mirror

when the love is not enough:
the conversation I never had with billie holiday

for billie holiday and black womben whose curled frames have cried
and who continue to shake from solitude overwhelming
for karen panzani

when late at night your curled frame cried
you wept for faith broken
shook from solitude overwhelming
I begged for arms stretched welcoming
not lies in tin pan alley cries
billie I miss you
I miss loneliness profound

I miss the sun smiling at dawn
this enigma of attraction
I am cutting you in two you said
cutting you open to put a river in
cutting you in two and washing everything away
washing you clean
washing you open
billie you open
I still miss you

and I know it's safe to leave the familiar
late-night visits

broken havens
safe promises
it hurts on the other side
how familiar to leave the familiar
no more late-night visits
late-night visits
billie I miss you

billie. I jumped from seventy-five dollars a week to
a thousand dollars a week at café society in manhattan
I was flaming it in the day
the cadillac
the green mink coat
the sex
the booze
the drugs
the hate
misery was mine for sure
when I died in '59
it wasn't any of that stuff though
my heart just gave out
broken I suppose
all them damn love songs

billie. it's cold. I cannot see silhouettes
my voice screams your betrayal
my faith is shaken
no broken
a companion to this misery

d'bi. I would rather have you billie

billie. yeah I know i'm late again
ain't no show gonna start without me
you hear
not without me
my pretty hair
I don't care

d'bi. like drowning the weight of this love resuscitates me
our beings too light and grace for this place

billie. when I got outta jail in '49
I played carnegie hall
thousands of people came to see me
everybody was happy
everybody except me
I knew they was only coming to see how high I was

billie. nobody sings the word hunger like I do. or the word love

d'bi. madness encroaches. a phantom stillness. be still. these words lie

billie. why lie? william dufty was offering me
some money to do my autobiography
I told him some trash. he made up some trash
I told him what he wanted to hear
and he heard what he thought people wanted to hear
who wants to know a real story of a black womban anyways
everybody thought they knew me
so it really didn't matter

d'bi. *lady sings the blues* does not soothe my soul

billie. do you wanna know how I got these gardenias in my hair

d'bi. don't change the subject billie
left with this bio-myth-o-graphy in hand
a silhouette
I long to know you
I cannot know you
my faith is shaken
how do I handle a faith broken

billie. look kid

d'bi. I am not upset. I am sad

billie. he needed a book
I needed money
that's all there is to it

d'bi. I miss the sun smiling at dawn
this enigma of attraction
like drowning the weight of our love resus-stifles me
I am cutting you in two you said
you said I cut you in two
cut you in two
put a river in
and wash you clean
wash you clean

billie. so I was telling you about the gardenias
one day I was inna hurry to get on stage
I was using a hot iron to curl my hair
I damn near burnt all of it out on the other side
it hurts on the other side
had to cover it with something
there were some gardenias on the table
ain't that a story if there ever was one
hey kid
hey kid
gone
just like the rest of them
when the love is not enough

d'bi. late at night your curled frame cried
wept for faith broken
shook from solitude overwhelming
my arms stretched welcoming

billie. you see kid
when you on the road
and you trying to please so many
and they want you to sing this way
and that way
bend this note and that note
and give all the good feeling

billie. I toured with count basie
and they fired me
said I sang too slow
I toured with artie shaw
and they fired me
said I was too artistic

billie. and one day I just can't do it

d'bi. I remembered you yesterday
wrapped in gardenias
floating on angel dust
hunger
love
quenched by your long-time lover
jack daniel

I remembered you tomorrow
wrapped in gardenias
the sun smiling at dawn
an enigma of attraction
you apparent
my own reflection a lie
billie
I love you

(post)colonial blues

no place
to place dis cunt
and spirit
no man. woman. animal. plant
inanimate object
no dildos
vibrators. fingers. tongue
nothing
no I don't want to spread my fucking legs
not from behind. not missionary
not in my mouth. not in my eyes
men and women
disgust me

where are the people who know how to fuck
fuck through the rape
violence. molestation
fuck so I like it again
for the first time

why your dick inside me
colonizer

duality on a binary fetus (ii)
for michelle

queer
fear
womban
unveiled fringes without choice

audre lorde

hypocrisies
contradictions
juxtapositions

running naked
black breasts
hanging low
mothering male children

I un-know and know
myself
daily

blood orange

it is a harvest moon
of chance
pregnant and powerful
that sits glowing
behind her lover's left ear

she peers at the moon's roundness
wanting to wear her own
changing body
becoming full
as unapologetically

flirting at the moon
then with her lover's eyes
and back again
she can't resist comparing the three
their depths
their beauties
sit struggling
in the mystic waters of a moon-oasis.

a harvest moon
bleeds like a blood orange
you peel patiently
wrapping your mouth

around its fleshy surface
allowing your teeth and tongue and lips
to press and pull into it
until you separate parts of the whole
not violent
not forceful
and those separated parts become
what makes you a complete human being

sitting there
her own blood
pulsing
with imperfect cell(ve)s
coursing like she wished her heart would flow
urgent and steady
but instead
her heart beats like a pounding river
mashing callously against stones and shells
on a hot kingston-river banking

in/consistent and in/love
she completes
the full moon harvest
of herself and of…

(w)hole

my eyes
black holes of
figments of construction
dance
flicker like desperate stars
fighting the inevitable dawn
eager and frustrated

if my stare stalks yearnings
it is because of an unruly memory
auction blocks and divided destinies
womben here men there
children no where

and yes
I feel I may not survive
another
loss of you

to another place
not here

love speak

what language have I
to transcend the treachery
of miscommunication
should poetry give name to
thought
then courage births revolushunaries
of love
these silent spaces sprout seeds
for a mute beginning
and I am left at the end of the circle
contemplating running the track of
my choices yet again

breathless
from fear

praise song for mengesha (i)

elelelelelelelelelelelelelelelelelele

in one far place
across the land
there lives a storyteller womban
whose name is weyni gebrehiwot elelta mengesha
weynie
weynie
weynie
weynie
whose name is weyni gebrehiwot elelta mengesha

meselu gebrehiwot jayle
ase unto you
so the ancestors say
for opening the prophet's passageway
to bring us weynie

from far and wide
the village come
to celebrate your phoenix moon
we've brought you jewels
of love and praise
your name is weynie
weynie
weynie

weynie
weynie
your name is weyni gebrehiwot elelta mengesha

should kindness be a river strong
we'd name her in your honour today
because like the nile
your goodness is long
from here unto gabon

your eyes a mirror of darkness and light
your lips chant down humanity's plight
your thoughts and actions fighting for the right
of those whom others deny

reborn of fire seven times four
the ancestors return once more
channelling their wisdom through your core
the village waits by your door
weynie
weynie
weynie
weynie
your name is weyni gebrehiwot elelta mengesha

oh weynie we love you so
a storyteller whose stories show
pure honesty and integrity
brown earth in you love grows

today we speak our promise of trust·
we will keep you as you have kept us
for all your days spread forth on this earth
your name is weynie

weynie
weynie
weynie
weynie
your name is weyni gebrehiwot elelta mengesha

praise song for mengesha (ii)

diasporic dawta
dance
deep
diasporic dawta
dance deep down
diasporic dawta
dance
deep
diasporic dawta
dance deep down
crowned
crowned
crowned

untitled (ii)

change is a fertile soil
in it
I plant my future

little sistah
for fadesha michelle alexander

little sistah
you reflect the truth I am becoming
dark dawta wading through waters of
self-love and self-knowing
the work ahead is the work of the past
honour life's lessons in cycles
and you will walk past the sameness
of our misgivings
not having to reinvent the wheel of experience
but carrying on your own rolls of wisdom
passed down through mother ancestor
great-grandmother grandmother
and mother

little sistah
I look to you for guidance
already rooted in my chosen step
new trees
share branches through which the sunlight
illuminates
casting a cool shade of
how can we do this differently the next time around
you are the universe's way of blessing herself
another opportunity on this gift of life

little sistah
a wise one once told me
courage is not to live without fear
courage is to hold fear as your most intimate lover
and in so doing
act with integrity respecting your fears
and they will respect you

little sistah
this is your road
walk it well

delusions and grandeur

yes this place
is
past pains
one hundred years

what do you want
whatever
are you hungry
not really
what can I make
anything

the kitchen sinks

where is poetry now
a great wordsmith
with nothing to say

seven generashuns
for the ones yet to come

(i)
from my belly bursts
forest fires of redemption
quenching these beasts of burden
and salvation
triggers retraumatize like a broken-trust-machine

you make me want to rethink
self-love
reactualize it
theorize and philosophize it
spiritualize it
until transformed
it wraps herself around you
being the truth we are

I want to come again
come again to the table, our temple
with yet another offering
a deeper version of self
this impulse to run and start fires
concrete jungle fires
that mirror this unruly blaze
aflamed
in my heart

(ii)
a warrior-angel to love this little black girl
and one to love this little black boy
into seven generashuns

love each other well… if you do nothing else
it will start fires
healing seven more to come

(iii)
who will hold her hand
little black girl
and take her to the well
in it stares her reflection
a blue pyramid

little black boy who will take your hands
and hold them in their own
then place them on your beating heart
a celebrashun you were born

then who will show you both
how to love
yourselves and your children
your lovers and friends
who will show you to spread that love
beyond your destiny's end

who will be patient enough to help you cry through growth
and not punish you wickedly for falling in your step
who will hold your trust so dear
and not break it
over a back
refusing to bend

who will change your his and her-story
so dis dysfunction ends…

an olive branch

cry
cry when love's labour loses herself
in a sea of habitual passions
flamed anger
red and scorching
blinding the bonds of integrity
you and your lover
pledged by the riverside

cry
cry for the deferred nightmares
posing as dreams
as pompous and purple as
nine eggplants to oya—defender of womban
for my dreams are drying and dying
raisins that will not sweeten my palate nor my pussy

cry
cry to ochun yemonja and elegua
whose intervention stands like an ancestorship
of berlin walls and global warmings
in an age of the end
our love signalled a beginning
and I dare to pluck my heart from her resting place
a sleeping giant now awake and hungry

I am the future of you. I am your past. I am the deep swelling of potential coming. I am water. I am breath. I am the crone. older than blood bleeding wounds which never dry for I am water.

rivers and other blackness between us
for gryphen and moon

who among us carry the sage-secrets of loving?
who among us carry the sage-secrets of loving?

what elders and children
walk with old-time knowledge
of a courageous love
an unapologetic love
an uncompromising love
a healing love
tell me who
and I will sit studently
by the rivers of their feet
washing away all the unknowing I have come to know
relearning a language of integrity honesty and compassion
scribed on our heart's tongue
by the ancients
whom I have forgotten

somewhere between a dream and a time-less-ness
across di ocean waters
black sons and dawtahs
black moddahs and faadahs
black auntie uncle sistah and breddah
stretch love fabric

thick and thin
suh now we trodding
trying to heal dese scars
of broken fibre
dat stick up inna wi like macka

who among us carry the sage-secrets?

what elders and children
walk with old-time knowledge
of a compassionate love
an unapologetic love
an uncompromising love
a healing love
tell me who
and I will sit studently
by the rivers of their feet
washing away all the unknowing I have come to know
relearning a language of integrity honesty passion
a language scribed on our heart's tongue
by those ancients
whom we have forgotten

black lover friend
forgive us for not having loved you relentlessly
in all cases fear has been our worst enemy

were fear not here
I would kiss you

and feed you food from my mouth
stop you from aching and share a smile
maybe even wait by the roadside for a while

were fear not here
I would give name to unnamed
spaces of accountability
and responsibility
that flow like rivers between us
sometimes silent but always deep

were fear not here
the full-moon radiance of your
vulnerable warrior spirit
washing over me like the sun
bathed in blackness
could mirror and shine brilliantly

but who among us carry the sage-secrets?

what elders and children
walk with the old-time knowledge
of a courageous love
an unapologetic love
an uncompromising love
a healing love
tell me who
and I will sit studently
by the rivers of their feet

washing away all the unknowing I have come to know
relearning a language of integrity honesty passion
scribed on our heart's tongue
by those ancients
whom we all have forgotten

black lover friend
I cannot promise to love you fearlessly
but I will love you courageously
in spite of my fear
I will love you compassionately
honestly
and with integrity

this is a healing love
rebranching herself like the iroko tree
roots reaching beyond
wounds of yesterday
arms outstretched to the promise of tomorrow

black lover friend
you and I
stand firm in now

About the Artist

Suritah Wignall (www.sweetlikemangoe.com) is a brilliant emerging Torontonian artist whose work examines the relationship between the mind, body, and spirit—particularly as they relate to the exploration of beauty, life, and culture in the African diaspora.

Thank You

ase to the ancestors. to the orishas. and to the spirit guides. ase mama nature for another round on the merry go round. mom. moon. family. mentors. mentees. lovers. friends. strangers. ase.